For 1994.01.25

Dear Cher
Love Ol
Enjoy!

# THAT SPECIAL

## *Woman*

*Getting Older,*
*Getting Better*

EDITED BY LOIS L. KAUFMAN

Designed by Michel Design
Illustrated by Grace De Vito

**P** PETER PAUPER PRESS, INC.
WHITE PLAINS · NEW YORK

Copyright © 1994
Peter Pauper Press, Inc.
202 Mamaroneck Avenue
White Plains, NY  10601
All rights reserved
ISBN 0-88088-869-5
Printed in Singapore
7  6  5  4  3  2  1

*Jacket background painting by Grace De Vito*

# Introduction

As Dorothy Canfield Fisher said, *One of the many things nobody ever tells you about middle age is that it's such a nice change from being young.*

We women are discovering that the young years are not necessarily the best years. Freedom from the responsibilities and worries of earlier years brings a welcome opportunity to venture into new fields that never seemed to be available to us before.

New perspectives can bring new challenges and experiences, and new successes. We don't worry so much about failure, because we have learned to persevere. *There's many a good tune played on an old fiddle!*

Life is unpredictable, so let's enjoy it, and make the most of every minute.

L. L. K.

$\mathcal{T}$o be somebody you must last.

RUTH GORDON

$\mathcal{A}$ woman past forty should make up her *mind* to be young, not her face.

BILLIE BURKE

$\mathcal{M}$ost human beings today waste some twenty-five to thirty years of their lives before they break through the actual and conventional lies which surround them.

ISADORA DUNCAN

$\mathcal{T}$he hardest years in life are those between ten and seventy.

HELEN HAYES, *at age 83*

$\mathcal{T}$here's nothing so sad as a 55-year-old orphan.

ELLA GRASSO, *after her parents' deaths*

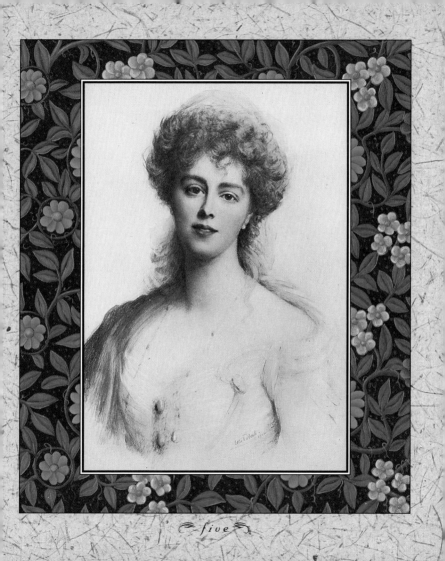

five

$\mathcal{Y}$ou'll be old and you never lived, and you kind of feel silly to lie down and die and to never have lived, to have been a job chaser and never have lived.

GERTRUDE STEIN

$\mathcal{A}$ll things are possible until they are proved impossible—and even the impossible may only be so, as of now.

PEARL S. BUCK

$\mathcal{I}$ think of age as a great universalizing force. It's the only thing we all have in common. It doesn't begin when you collect your social security benefits. Aging begins with the moment of birth, and it ends only when life itself has ended. Life is a continuum; only, we—in our stupidity and blindness—have chopped it up into little pieces and kept all those little pieces separate.

MAGGIE KUHN

*S*ecurity is mostly a superstition. It does not exist in nature…. Life is either a daring adventure or nothing.

HELEN KELLER

*M*y grandmother started walking five miles a day when she was sixty. She's ninety-seven now, and we don't know where the hell she is.

ELLEN DEGENERES

*A*ge puzzles me. I thought it was a quiet time. My seventies were interesting and fairly serene, but my eighties are passionate. I grow more intense as I age.

FLORIDA SCOTT-MAXWELL

*I* pray that I may be all that [my mother] would have been had she lived in an age when women could aspire and achieve and daughters are cherished as much as sons.

JUSTICE RUTH BADER GINSBURG

*W*hen men reach their sixties and retire, they go to pieces. Women just go right on cooking.

GAIL SHEEHY

*T*he people have kept me a star for 30-some years because there's a truth to my work and that's what they get. And if I keep telling the truth, I can't get hurt.

BARBRA STREISAND

*I* have found that age is a careless jailer. There are hours, days, even weeks, when it doesn't seem to check up on you much. During those times, you are the same whizzy you have always been, in some ways better. What I believe is that you keep from going down the drain by using whatever you've got to work with, working like a maniac and hoping everything will come out okay. It frequently does.

HELEN GURLEY BROWN

*I'm* lucky I'm married to a wealthy, successful, generous man, but I'm not dependent on him. I have my earning power, my own ability to maintain my life by myself. And that's true liberation. The sooner women figure that out, the better. We're liberated not by laws but by being self-sufficient, self-reliant and liking ourselves.

GEORGETTE MOSBACHER

*In* youth we learn; in age we understand.

MARIE VON EBNER ESCHENBACH

*len*

$\mathcal{L}$ife has got to be lived—that's all there is to it. At seventy, I would say the advantage is that you take life more calmly. You know that this, too, shall pass!

ELEANOR ROOSEVELT

$\mathcal{N}$othing in life just happens. You have to have the stamina to meet obstacles and overcome them. To struggle.

GOLDA MEIR

$\mathcal{I}$ was thinking, 45—that's middle age. Well, I'm going to have the best damn middle age anybody ever had.

LAURA Z. HOBSON

$\mathcal{O}$nce you have been confronted with a life-and-death situation, trivia no longer matters. Your perspective grows and you live at a deeper level. There's no time for pettiness.

MARGARETTA (HAPPY) ROCKEFELLER

*I*'m not embarrassed to be with a younger man, except when I drop him off at school.

ANGIE DICKINSON

*I* refuse to admit I'm more than fifty-two, even if that does make my sons illegitimate.

LADY ASTOR

*I* think of myself as thirty-two. But when I was thirty-two, I felt a hundred.

BEATRICE WOOD, *on turning 100*

*W*hat you have become is the price you paid to get what you used to want.

MIGNON McLAUGHLIN

*O*ne's prime is elusive. You little girls, when you grow up, must be on the alert to recognize your prime at whatever time of your life it may occur. You must then live it to the full.

MURIEL SPARK, *THE PRIME OF MISS JEAN BRODIE*

*O*h roses for the flush of youth, and laurel for the perfect prime, but pluck an ivy branch for me grown old before my time.

CHRISTINA ROSSETTI

*A*t fifty, I think I may be growing up at last.

ALI MCGRAW

*M*y feeling about aging is that some of my favorite people—most of my heroes—are over 75. For myself, personally, I've always felt 40. I never felt 16 and dewy and new. So recently I've felt like myself, comfortable.

MERYL STREEP

*To* insist on staying young is to grow old with pessimism, like a wine which little by little turns to vinegar.

MOTHER OF PRINCESS GRACE OF MONACO

*There* are compensations for growing older. One is the realization that to be sporting isn't at all necessary. It is a great relief to reach this stage of wisdom.

CORNELIA OTIS SKINNER

*I'm* not afraid of old age—it's nothing to fear. I will be a very wise and serious old lady. As I get older, I get quieter, because now I know myself better.

SOPHIA LOREN

*I* never allow myself to be bored, because boredom is aging. If you live in the past you grow old, and dull, and dusty. It's very nice, of course, to be young and beautiful; but there are other qualities, thank God.

MARIE TEMPEST

$\mathcal{I}$m having a glorious old age. One of my greatest delights is that I have outlived most of my opposition.

MAGGIE KUHN

$\mathcal{O}$lder women are like aging strudels—the crust may not be so lovely, but the filling has come at last into its own.

ROBERT FARRAR CAPON

$\mathcal{I}$ have everything I had twenty years ago, only it's all a little bit lower.

GYPSY ROSE LEE

$\mathcal{W}$e no longer look forward to letting go at thirty. There is no thought of aging gracefully at forty. At fifty, we are faced with a prospect of daily regimens to soften our skin and tighten our thighs. The end result of all this is that those of us who failed to look like Brooke Shields at seventeen can now fail to look like Victoria Principal at thirty-three and like Linda Evans at forty-one and like Sophia Loren at fifty.

ELLEN GOODMAN

$\mathcal{L}$ook out. I'm driving again.

BARBARA BUSH, *at age 68*

$\mathcal{W}$ho wants to be around anyone who complains? It is so unpleasant. I believe in denial. Denial is a marvelous thing.

KITTY CARLISLE HART, *at age 83*

$\mathcal{I}$t is sad to grow old but nice to ripen.

BRIGITTE BARDOT

*seventeen*

$\mathscr{I}$am still trying to find out things about myself. I want to be more loving, more compassionate, because I have a tendency to be cut off and not allow feelings in, and it's something I really strive to change in myself.

BARBRA STREISAND

$\mathscr{T}$he process of maturing is an art to be learned, an effort to be sustained. By the age of fifty you have made yourself what you are, and if it is good, it is better than your youth.

MARYA MANNES

$\mathscr{M}$y dear, when you are my age you will realize that what you need is the maturer man.

LADY DIANA COOPER, *at age 86*

$\mathscr{W}$omen are most fascinating between the age of thirty-five and forty after they have won a few races and know how to pace themselves. Since few women ever pass forty, maximum fascination can continue indefinitely.

CHRISTIAN DIOR

*T*he woman who tells her age is either too young to have anything to lose or too old to have anything to gain.

CHINESE PROVERB

*Y*outh is the time of getting, middle age of improving, and old age of spending.

ANNE BRADSTREET

*M*y forties are the best time I have ever gone through.

ELIZABETH TAYLOR

*Y*outh lasts much longer than young people think.

COMTESSE DIANE

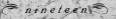

*My* daughters Zsa Zsa, Eva and Magda and I are like good wine—we improve with age.

JOLIE GABOR

*Pushing* forty? She's hanging onto it for dear life.

IVY COMPTON-BURNETT

*I* know I have the body of a weak and feeble woman; but I have the heart and stomach of a king, and of a King of England, too.

QUEEN ELIZABETH I, *at age 55*

$\mathcal{M}$y vigor, vitality and cheek repel me. I am the kind of woman I would run from.

LADY ASTOR

$\mathcal{B}$ut an old woman . . . is a person who has no sense of decency; if once she takes to living, the devil himself can't get rid of her.

FANNY BURNEY, *CECILIA*

$\mathcal{A}$n old man in the house is a burden; but an old woman in the house is a treasure.

TALMUD

$\mathcal{M}$id-50's is too young to settle for ashes if there's still fire in the furnace.

ANN LANDERS, *to a middle-aged woman in a celibate marriage*

*twenty two*

$\mathscr{W}$e've changed, and so will our friends. The truth is that all of us—divorcées, widows and those whose time has not yet come—are going to have more than one life to live. Sooner or later we discover that we only rent our happiness or unhappiness, we don't own it, and we'd better be prepared to move out on short notice, carrying our own suitcases at that. After all, who ever promised us perpetual care?

Joan Gould

$\mathscr{I}$t's life, isn't it? You plow ahead and make a hit. And you plow on and someone passes you. Then someone passes them. Time levels.

Katharine Hepburn

$\mathscr{T}$he last 100 years of my life have been filled with new things.

Lillian Postman, *age 108*

*I* think [bliss is] being surrounded by people you love. I don't think it's any more complicated than that.

ANITA RODDICK

*M*ake it a rule of life never to regret and never look back. Regret is an appalling waste of energy; you can't build on it; it is good only for wallowing in.

KATHERINE MANSFIELD

*T*he older one grows the more one likes indecency.

VIRGINIA WOOLF

*I*f you rest, you rust.

HELEN HAYES

*Age ain't nothin' but a number.* But age is other things, too. It is wisdom, if one has lived one's life properly. It is experience and knowledge. And it is getting to know all the ways the world turns, so that if you cannot turn the world the way you want, you can at least get out of the way so you won't get run over.

MIRIAM MAKEBA

*O*ld people do have sex and they have it a lot. They're just doing it a little more slowly, which, come to think of it, is not a bad thing.

ESTELLE GETTY

*W*hen one door of happiness closes, another opens; but often we look so long at the closed door that we do not see the one which has been opened for us.

HELEN KELLER

$\mathcal{A}$ young girl can get away with throwing on any old rag; an older woman has to have clothes of superior cut and fabric. What counts is neatness, neatness, neatness. Sloppiness adds years.

COCO CHANEL

$\mathcal{W}$hen we grow old, there can only be one regret—not to have given enough of ourselves.

ELEONORA DUSE

$\mathcal{T}$he great thing about getting older is that you don't lose all the other ages you've been.

MADELEINE L'ENGLE

$\mathcal{T}$ime is a fixed income and, as with any income, the real problem facing most of us is how to live successfully within our daily allotment.

MARGARET B. JOHNSTONE

$\mathcal{N}$o one grows old by living—only by losing interest in living.

MARIE BEYNON RAY

$\mathcal{N}$ow that they no longer have a woman at the helm [the United Kingdom] has a hell of a budget deficit.

MARGARET THATCHER

$\mathcal{L}$iving never wore one out so much as the effort not to live.

ANAÏS NIN

$\mathcal{H}$ow absurd and delicious it is to be in love with somebody younger than yourself. Everybody should try it.

BARBARA PYM, *A VERY PRIVATE EYE*

$\mathcal{A}$ge does not protect you from love. But love, to some extent, protects you from age.

JEANNE MOREAU

$\mathscr{I}$t is eleven years since I have seen my figure in a glass: the last reflexion I saw there was so disagreeable, I resolved to spare myself such mortifications for the future, and shall continue that resolution to my life's end. To indulge all pleasing amusements, and avoid all images that give disgust, is, in my opinion, the best method to attain or confirm health.

LADY MARY WORTLEY MONTAGU, *at age 68*

$\mathscr{T}$hirty-five is a very attractive age. London society is full of women of the very highest birth who have, of their own free choice, remained thirty-five for years.

OSCAR WILDE

$\mathscr{A}$ll one's life as a young woman one is on show, a focus of attention, people notice you. You set yourself up to be noticed and admired. And then, not expecting it, you become middle-aged and anonymous. No one notices you. You achieve a wonderful freedom. It is a positive thing. You can move about, unnoticed and invisible.

DORIS LESSING

*I* want to have more fun. I'm willing to take those chances now, you know, to live life to its fullest.

BARBRA STREISAND

*It* is so comic to hear oneself called old, even at ninety I suppose!

ALICE JAMES

*My* mother taught me that we all do the same routine things—work, eat, sleep, wash, have sex. What makes us different is how we do them.

DIANE VON FURSTENBERG

*In* a society rooted in a virtual cult to youth, the nature and circumstance of youth is often grossly distorted. But the nature of age is often invisible.

MARGARET RANDALL

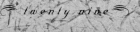

*F*ew women, I fear, have had such reason as I have to think the long sad years of youth were worth living for the sake of middle age.

GEORGE ELIOT

*T*he only reason I would take up jogging is so that I could hear heavy breathing again.

ERMA BOMBECK

*E*ndow the already established with money. Endow the woman who shows genius with time.

MARIA MITCHELL

*I* am at present in such health and such spirits, that when I recollect I am an old woman, I am astonished.

CATHERINE CLIVE, *at age 58*

*A* woman of sixty, like a girl of six, will run at the sound of wedding music.

JEWISH PROVERB

$\mathcal{T}$he bottom line, the ultimate wrinkle, is the integrity of the self. I wish I could face it down, but I can't. One must fight for one's self, even though the reward for waging that battle is often no more, but never less, than the cold consolation of integrity.

That's why I haven't gotten a face lift—so far.

MARY-LOU WEISMAN

$\mathcal{I}$ don't date much. One guy was so old he picked me up in a hearse.

JOAN RIVERS

$\mathcal{T}$he work I did, the proof of my ability, the establishment of my credibility, all were and still are the material on which I assess myself. I gave up my self-esteem twice in my life—once when I left retailing and put aside my role as a worker and, again, after I had my daughters, when I stayed too long out of the work force.

FRANCES LEAR

*It* costs me everything to write, which is really why it's at least rather poignant, if not ironic, when critics say, *Well, Maya Angelou has a new book and, of course, it's very good, but then she's a natural writer*. A *natural* writer is like being a *natural* open-heart surgeon.

MAYA ANGELOU

*From* birth to age eighteen, a girl needs good parents. From eighteen to thirty-five, she needs good looks. From thirty-five to fifty-five, she needs a good personality. From fifty-five on, she needs good cash.

SOPHIE TUCKER

*Women* whose identity depends more on their outsides than their insides are dangerous when they begin to age.

GLORIA STEINEM

*I* have always felt that a woman has the right to treat the subject of her age with ambiguity until, perhaps, she passes into the realm of over ninety. Then it is better she be candid with herself and with the world.

HELENA RUBINSTEIN

*W*hen you cease to make a contribution you begin to die.

ELEANOR ROOSEVELT

*T*here's a lot of information directed at and about youth, career making and being young mothers, but we must teach young women to see ahead 20 years. None of us can ward off the penalties of age, but we can learn to think ahead. We're so youth-oriented, we don't want to think about being 60 or 70.

LILLIAN HELLMAN

*O*ne of the many things nobody ever tells you about middle age is that it's such a nice change from being young.

DOROTHY CANFIELD FISHER

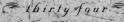

$\mathcal{N}$ature gives you the face you have at 20; it is up to you to merit the face you have at 50.

COCO CHANEL

$\mathcal{A}$t seventeen I was so enamored of life, of its vagaries, its soaring flights and precipitous depths, that I promised myself I would experience everything, stipulating no qualities good or bad, and it has pretty much all happened. Little more than I knew at seventeen do I surely know who I am at seventy-five.

KATE SIMON

$\mathcal{T}$he wise are neither young nor old—their physical age tells us nothing, any more than the generality of men can be divided between age and youth on the basis of their knowledge. The wise are always young in will and energy and old in experience and reflection.

FRANCES R. LISCHNER

*I* like living. I have sometimes been wildly, despairingly, acutely miserable, racked with sorrow, but through it all I still know quite certainly that just to be alive is a grand thing.

AGATHA CHRISTIE

*Y*ou don't stop being a girl because they give you a different number.

CAROL MATTHAU

*M*y sixty-sixth birthday, and I still have all my old energy and passion, the same acute sensitivity, and, people tell me, the same youthful appearance.

SOFIA TOLSTOY

*A*n archeologist is the best husband any woman can have: the older she gets, the more interested he is in her.

AGATHA CHRISTIE

*T*he really frightening thing about middle age is the knowledge that you'll grow out of it.

DORIS DAY

*M*y most successful achievement after reaching age 65 was becoming 66. And after that, it was getting to be 67, 68, and right up to where I am now, 82. My after-65 career has been as happy, as resultful, and as satisfying as my pre-65 period.

RUTH GORDON

*T*ime and trouble will tame an advanced young woman, but an advanced old woman is uncontrollable by any earthly force.

DOROTHY L. SAYERS

*T*he influence you exert is through your own life and what you've become yourself.

ELEANOR ROOSEVELT

*T*here is no such thing as an old woman. Any woman of any age, if she loves, if she is good, gives a man a sense of the infinite.

JULES MICHELET

*Y*ou gain strength, courage and confidence by every experience in which you really stop to look fear in the face…You must do the thing which you think you cannot do.

ELEANOR ROOSEVELT

$\mathcal{W}$e grow old more through indolence than through age.

CHRISTINA OF SWEDEN

$\mathcal{F}$or the ignorant, old age is as winter; for the learned, it is a harvest.

HASIDIC SAYING

$\mathcal{B}$ecoming a farmer—Type: Other; Land Owned: 90 acres; Status: Single; Sex: Female; Age: 50—has forced a competence upon me that I would never have had under other circumstances. And that, I realize as I lie on the creeper under my Chevy, has made me outrageously happy.

SUE HUBBELL

$\mathcal{L}$et me not forget that I am the daughter of a woman who bent her head, trembling, between the blades of a cactus, her wrinkled face full of ecstasy over the promise of a flower, a woman who herself never ceased to flower, untiringly, during three quarters of a century.

COLETTE

$\mathscr{I}$wasn't working to earn retirement, see. I was working 'cause I love to work. The work is my pleasure. I'm having so much *fun*.

PHYLLIS DILLER

$\mathscr{D}$on't be afraid your life will end; be afraid that it will never begin.

GRACE HANSEN

$\mathscr{T}$here's many a good tune played on an old fiddle.

PROVERB

$\mathscr{W}$omen may be the one group that grows more radical with age.

GLORIA STEINEM

$\mathscr{D}$iscussing how old you are is the temple of boredom.

RUTH GORDON

$\mathcal{W}$omen of all ages are finding they have political power.
There are more women voting than there are men. Women
have the power and the authority to bring up the issues
that concern them.

*P*erhaps middle age is, or should be, a period of shedding shells; the shell of ambition, the shell of material accumulations and possessions, the shell of the ego. Perhaps one can shed at this stage in life as one sheds in beach-living; one's pride, one's false ambitions, one's mask, one's armor.

ANNE MORROW LINDBERGH

*[A*merican women have been] liberated from the old-age syndrome. There are no *older women* in America today. Women are all young in mind, young in spirit; they can wear any kind of clothes.

HALSTON

*T*here is no cosmetic for beauty like happiness.

COUNTESS OF BLESSINGTON

*W*hat's the point? My face, shall we say, looks lived in.

AVA GARDNER, *on the question of lying about her age at 65*

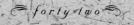

*I* view aging as a blessing. One of the things that frustrates me about modeling is that you're judged solely on how you look. When you get older, you're judged more on the person you are, and that's a great reward.

KATHY IRELAND

*Y*outh is not a time of life; it is a state of mind. People grow old only by deserting their ideals and by outgrowing the consciousness of youth…. The way to keep young is to keep your faith young. Keep your self-confidence young. Keep your hope young.

LUELLA F. PHELAN

*O*ne of the signs of passing youth is the birth of a sense of fellowship with other human beings as we take our place among them.

VIRGINIA WOOLF

*L*ife forms illogical patterns. It is haphazard and full of beauties which I try to catch as they fly by, for who knows whether any of them will ever return?

MARGOT FONTEYN

*O*ne thing life taught me—if you are interested, you never have to look for new interests. They come to you.

ELEANOR ROOSEVELT

*T*he secret of eternal youth is arrested development.

ALICE ROOSEVELT LONGWORTH

$\mathcal{A}$ letter from a lady who has described me in a French newspaper—*a noble lady with a shock of white hair*—Lord, are we as old as all that? I feel about six and a half.

VIRGINIA WOOLF

$\mathcal{P}$atience makes a woman beautiful in middle age.

ELLIOT PAUL

$\mathcal{T}$here are six myths about old age: 1. That it's a disease, a disaster. 2. That we are mindless. 3. That we are sexless. 4. That we are useless. 5. That we are powerless. 6. That we are all alike.

MAGGIE KUHN

$\mathcal{W}$hen Gloria Steinem turned fifty, she updated her famous line from forty. She said, *This is what fifty looks like.* With due apologies to the cult of midlife beauty, allow me two words: *Not necessarily.*

ELLEN GOODMAN

$\mathcal{T}$he primitive, physical, functional pattern of the morning of life, the active years before forty or fifty, is outlived. But there is still the afternoon opening up, which one can spend not in the feverish pace of the morning but in having time at last for those intellectual, cultural, and spiritual activities that were pushed aside in the heat of the race.

ANNE MORROW LINDBERGH

$\mathcal{T}$he sentimentalist ages far more quickly than the person who loves his work and enjoys new challenges.

LILY LANGTRY

$\mathcal{M}$ost good women are hidden treasures who are only safe because nobody looks for them.

DOROTHY PARKER

*T*here is only one solution if old age is not to be an absurd parody of our former life, and that is to go on pursuing ends that give our existence a meaning— devotion to individuals, to groups or to causes, social, political, intellectual or creative work…. One's life has value so long as one attributes value to the life of others, by means of love, friendship, indignation, compassion.

SIMONE DE BEAUVOIR

*Y*ou have to invent and reinvent yourself. I keep reinventing myself as I grow. I take more chances and stick my neck out…

GEORGETTE MOSBACHER

*D*iscipline—in every way.

BROOKE ASTOR, *explaining her longevity*

*W*e older people need to accept ourselves at the age we are.

HELEN GURLEY BROWN

*W*hen the grandmothers of today hear the word *Chippendales*, they don't think of chairs.

JEAN KERR

*W*hat's needed [after divorce] is reality, and the way to get it is to write out your own checks to the landlord, the telephone company and Consolidated Edison. After a little prodding, it will eventually dawn on these people that if you can write real checks you must be a real person, and they will begin not only to accept your money but to send you bills—bills made out in your name.

   That's reality, and it's heaven.

ANN P. HARRIS

*I* think I'm in love…. Someone my age would fall in love, forty-five and in love, can you imagine?

ISABEL ALLENDE

*L*ife begins at forty.

SOPHIE TUCKER

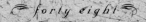

*I*f you want a thing well done, get a couple of old broads to do it.

BETTE DAVIS

*N*o matter how old a mother is, she watches her middle-aged children for signs of improvement.

FLORIDA SCOTT-MAXWELL

*O*ne of the few advantages to not being beautiful is that one usually gets better-looking as one gets older; I am, in fact, at this very moment gaining my looks.

NORA EPHRON

*I*f things get better with age, then I'm approaching magnificent.

ANONYMOUS

*Q*uite a few women told me, one way or another, that they thought it was sex, not youth, that's wasted on the young.

JANET HARRIS

*O*ld age, believe me, is a good and pleasant time. It is true that you are quietly shouldered off the stage, but then you are given such a comfortable front seat as spectator, and if you have really played your part you are more content to sit down and watch.

JANE ELLEN HARRISON

*I* believe that the sign of maturity is accepting deferred gratification.

PEGGY CAHN

*fifty one*

$\mathscr{I}$ look back on my life like a good day's work; it was done and I am satisfied with it.

GRANDMA MOSES

$\mathscr{A}$ much more effective and lasting method of face-lifting than surgical technique is happy thinking, new interests, and outdoor exercise.

SARA MURRAY JORDAN

**Reporter:** What does it feel like to be a woman Prime Minister?
**Margaret Thatcher:** I don't know. I've never experienced the contrary.

$\mathscr{O}$ld age is like a plane flying through a storm. Once you are aboard there is nothing you can do.

GOLDA MEIR

$\mathcal{A}$s I see it, there is not much difference between being sixty-three and fifty-three: whereas when I was fifty-three I felt at a staggering distance from forty-three.

SIMONE DE BEAUVOIR

$\mathcal{A}$ beautiful lady is an accident of nature. A beautiful old lady is a work of art.

LOUIS NIZER

$\mathcal{U}$neducated clever women, who have seen much of the world, are in middle life so much the most cultured part of the community. They have been saved from this horrible burden of inert ideas.

A. N. WHITEHEAD

$\mathcal{I}$t's not how old you are, but how you are old.

MARIE DRESSLER

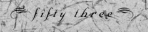
fifty three

*L*ife was meant to be lived, and curiosity must be kept alive. One must never, for whatever reason, turn his back on life.

ELEANOR ROOSEVELT

*S*ometimes I just go [to the beauty salon] for an estimate.

PHYLLIS DILLER

*I*t isn't just older women who get depressed checking out the before and after portraits of women who injected collagen into their laugh lines. The baby-boom generation of women, raised on youth and fitness, has turned forty, facing a future of Optifast, aerobics and sunblock.

ELLEN GOODMAN

*A*h well, perhaps one has to be very old before one learns how to be amused rather than shocked.

PEARL S. BUCK

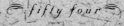

$\mathcal{I}$m not living the last third of my life as if it's already over. People live their lives as if the first two-thirds were all there is.

FAITH SEIDENBERG

$\mathcal{F}$or the last third of life there remains only work. It alone is always stimulating, rejuvenating, exciting and satisfying.

KÄTHE KOLLWITZ

$\mathcal{I}$m alone, free.

ISABEL ALLENDE

$\mathcal{M}$y life? It gets better all the time. What would be the point of getting older if you didn't get better—in every way?

MARLO THOMAS

# *I'M NOT YOUNG ANY MORE, AND*

*It's time for me.*

*I feel wiser.*

*I feel calmer, more at peace with myself and the world.*

*I count my blessings.*

*I'm more open to new experiences.*

*I value being comfortable.*

*I have fewer delusions.*

*I'm less concerned with what other people think.*

*I'm free, I can fly!*